HR STAMPED WAYS TO SAY THINGS I CAN'T SAY OUT LOUD AT WORK

(OFFICIALLY APPROVED)

Welcome to the Office Jungle

Congratulations! You've picked up this book, which means you're either trapped in a soul-crushing office job or you're shopping for someone who is. Either way, welcome to the club where we all pretend to care about "synergy" while secretly plotting our escape to a beach somewhere.

This book is for everyone who's ever sat through a three-hour meeting that could've been an email, smiled through gritted teeth at their micromanaging boss, or wondered if "circle back" is actually a form of torture banned by the Geneva Convention. It's for those brave souls who've mastered the art of saying "per my last email" when they really mean "can you fucking read?"

So pour yourself that third cup of terrible office coffee, minimize your actual work tabs, and enjoy this guide to surviving corporate America without getting fired. Remember: we're all in this together, separately, in our individual cubicles, pretending to be busy.

1. The Morning Check-In

"Why the hell are you asking me what I'm working on? It's the same shit I was working on yesterday when you asked me this exact same question."

WHAT HR WANTS YOU TO SAY

"I'm continuing to make excellent progress on the initiatives we discussed yesterday. I'd be happy to provide you with a detailed status update."

THE CORPORATE DICTIONARY

Check-in (n.): A daily ritual where managers cosplay as caring leaders while employees practice their poker faces.

2. The Reply-All Disaster

"WHO THE FUCK KEEPS HITTING REPLY ALL?
We don't all need to know that you'll be five
minutes late to the meeting, Brad!"

WHAT HR WANTS YOU TO SAY

"Just a friendly reminder that using 'Reply'
instead of 'Reply All' helps keep everyone's
inbox manageable and ensures important
messages don't get lost."

THE CORPORATE DICTIONARY

Reply-All-ocalypse (n.): The digital
equivalent of shouting in a library, but
somehow more annoying and affecting 200
people simultaneously.

3. The Deadline Surprise

"You want this by when?! Did you just pull this deadline out of your ass? Time doesn't work that way!"

"I want to ensure we deliver the highest quality work. Could we discuss the timeline to make sure we can meet your expectations?"

Deadline (n.): A randomly generated date designed to test the limits of human endurance and coffee consumption.

4. The Pointless Meeting

"This meeting is so pointless, I'm losing brain cells just sitting here. I could've been productive instead."

WHAT HR WANTS YOU TO SAY

"I'm wondering if we might be able to accomplish our objectives more efficiently through email or a brief document?"

THE CORPORATE DICTIONARY

Meetingnesia (n.): The phenomenon of forgetting everything discussed in a meeting the moment you leave the conference room.

5. The Micromanager

"Back off! I know how to do my job. That's why you hired me, remember? Or did you forget that part?"

WHAT HR WANTS YOU TO SAY

"I appreciate your guidance. I work best when I have some autonomy to implement the strategies we've discussed."

THE CORPORATE DICTIONARY

Micromanagement (n.): The art of hiring talented people and then preventing them from doing the job you hired them for.

8

6. The Vague Feedback

YOUR INNER VOICE

"What the fuck does 'make it pop more' even mean? Use your words like an adult!"

WHAT HR WANTS YOU TO SAY

"Could you help me understand your vision better? Perhaps you could share some specific examples of what you're looking for?"

THE CORPORATE DICTIONARY

Pop (v.): A meaningless directive that translates to "I don't know what I want, but I'll know it when I see it."

7. The Credit Thief

"That was MY idea, you piece of shit! I literally said that exact thing in last week's meeting!"

"I'm so glad you're championing this initiative! As we discussed last week, I'm excited to see how we can implement this together."

THE CORPORATE DICTIONARY

Collaboration (n.): A process where one person does all the work and another person takes all the credit.

8. The Instant Message Bombardment

"Can you stop pinging me every five seconds? I'm not your personal Google!"

WHAT HR WANTS YOU TO SAY

"I'm currently focused on a high-priority task. Could we schedule some time to discuss your questions all at once?"

THE CORPORATE DICTIONARY

Slackluster (adj.): The feeling of dread when you see 47 unread Slack notifications after a 10-minute bathroom break.

9. The Open Office Hell

"I can hear everyone's conversation, smell everyone's lunch, and I haven't had a coherent thought in three hours!"

WHAT HR WANTS YOU TO SAY

"I'm finding it a bit challenging to concentrate today. Would it be possible to book a quiet room for some focused work time?"

THE CORPORATE DICTIONARY

Open-plan (adj.): An architectural concept designed by someone who clearly hates productivity and human happiness.

10. The Buzzword Bonanza

"If you say 'synergy' one more time, I'm going to lose it. Speak like a normal human!"

WHAT HR WANTS YOU TO SAY

"I think I understand the concept. Could you help me understand how this applies specifically to our current project?"

THE CORPORATE DICTIONARY

Synergy (n.): A word used when you want to sound smart but have absolutely nothing meaningful to say.

11. The Last-Minute Request

"Are you fucking kidding me? You need this in an hour? What have you been doing all week?"

WHAT HR WANTS YOU TO SAY

"I want to make sure I can deliver quality work. Given the short timeline, what are the absolute must-haves versus nice-to-haves?"

THE CORPORATE DICTIONARY

Urgent (adj.): A classification applied to tasks that someone forgot about until the last possible moment.

12. The Conference Call Chaos

"Can everyone please mute their damn mics? I don't need to hear your dog, your kids, and your toilet flushing!"

WHAT HR WANTS YOU TO SAY

"Just a quick reminder to please mute when not speaking. It'll help ensure everyone can hear the discussion clearly."

THE CORPORATE DICTIONARY

Mute (v.): A button that 75% of meeting participants are physically incapable of locating.

13. The Mandatory Fun

"I'd rather stick needles in my eyes than go to another forced team-building event. This isn't fun; it's torture with snacks."

WHAT HR WANTS YOU TO SAY

"I appreciate the effort to bring the team together. Would it be possible to explore some alternative team-building options?"

THE CORPORATE DICTIONARY

Team-building (n.): Organized activities that prove your coworkers are just as awkward outside the office as they are inside it.

14. The Email Chain From Hell

"Why am I CC'd on this? This has nothing to do with me! Stop dragging me into your drama!"

WHAT HR WANTS YOU TO SAY

"Thanks for keeping me in the loop. Feel free to remove me from the chain if my input is no longer needed."

THE CORPORATE DICTIONARY

CC (V.): To involve innocent bystanders in email warfare they never asked to be part of.

15. The Zoom Fatigue

"If I have to stare at my own face in another video call, I'm going to scream. And no, I don't want to turn on my camera."

WHAT HR WANTS YOU TO SAY

"I'm experiencing some technical difficulties with my camera today. I'll participate via audio to ensure a smooth meeting."

THE CORPORATE DICTIONARY

Zoompathy (n.): The complete emotional exhaustion from pretending to be engaged while staring at a grid of faces on a screen.

16. The Office Temperature Wars

"It's either Antarctic winter or Death Valley in here. Can we pick a temperature that doesn't require survival gear?"

WHAT HR WANTS YOU TO SAY

"I've noticed the temperature fluctuates quite a bit. Could we explore finding a comfortable middle ground for everyone?"

THE CORPORATE DICTIONARY

Thermostat (n.): An office device that exists solely to create conflict between coworkers who run hot and those who run cold.

17. The Printer Problems

"This fucking printer has one job—ONE JOB—and it can't even do that without having an existential crisis!"

WHAT HR WANTS YOU TO SAY

"The printer seems to be experiencing some technical difficulties. Has anyone had success with troubleshooting it?"

THE CORPORATE DICTIONARY

PC-Load-Letter (n.): An error message designed by Satan himself to test the limits of human sanity.

18. The Performance Review Prep

"You want me to rate myself? Fine. I'm fucking amazing at pretending to care about this job. Five stars."

WHAT HR WANTS YOU TO SAY

"I'm looking forward to discussing my contributions this year and exploring opportunities for professional growth."

THE CORPORATE DICTIONARY

Self-evaluation (n.): An exercise in creative writing where you describe your mediocre year as a series of groundbreaking achievements.

19. The Office Birthday Party

"Great, another awkward gathering where we pretend to care about someone we barely talk to. Pass the sad cake."

"How thoughtful to celebrate our team members! I'll definitely stop by to wish them well."

Office-cake (n.): A dessert that tastes like obligation and frosted disappointment.

20. The Brainstorming Session

"Oh good, another session where we write stupid ideas on sticky notes and pretend they're genius. Kill me now."

"I'm excited to contribute to our ideation process. Shall we establish some parameters to guide our creative thinking?"

Brainstorm (v.): To generate 99 terrible ideas in hopes that one might accidentally be useful.

21. The Commute Conversation

"No, I don't want to hear about your commute. We all sat in traffic. It sucked. Move on."

"Sounds like you had quite the journey this morning! Hope the rest of your day goes more smoothly."

Commute (n.): Daily proof that hell is real and it's located between your home and office.

22. The "Quick Question"

"There's no such thing as a quick question. This is going to eat up my entire afternoon, isn't it?"

WHAT HR WANTS YOU TO SAY

"Of course! I have about 10 minutes right now, or we could schedule time to discuss it thoroughly."

THE CORPORATE DICTIONARY

Quick-question (n.): A lie told by people who are about to monopolize the next 45 minutes of your life.

23. The Office Kitchen Etiquette

"Who the hell microwaves fish in an office? Are you trying to make enemies?"

WHAT HR WANTS YOU TO SAY

"Just a friendly reminder that strong-smelling foods can be challenging in our shared space. Thanks for being considerate!"

THE CORPORATE DICTIONARY

Microwave (n.): An office appliance that doubles as a weapon of mass disgust when used incorrectly.

24. The Calendar Invite Spam

"Stop sending me calendar invites for shit I don't need to attend! My calendar looks like a game of Tetris!"

WHAT HR WANTS YOU TO SAY

"I want to ensure I'm using my time effectively. Could you help me understand my role in this meeting?"

THE CORPORATE DICTIONARY

Calendar-bombing (v.): The act of filling someone's schedule with meetings to create the illusion of productivity.

25. The "Constructive" Criticism

"That's not constructive criticism; that's just you being an asshole with extra words."

WHAT HR WANTS YOU TO SAY

"I appreciate your feedback. Could you provide some specific examples so I can better understand how to improve?"

THE CORPORATE DICTIONARY

Constructive (adj.): A word added before "criticism" to make insults sound professional.

26. The Overtime Expectations

"No, I can't stay late again. I have a life outside this hellhole. Remember those? Lives?"

WHAT HR WANTS YOU TO SAY

"I'm committed to meeting our deadlines. Let's discuss how to prioritize tasks within regular working hours."

THE CORPORATE DICTIONARY

Work-life-balance (n.): A mythical concept like unicorns, but less believable.

27. The "Circle Back" Loop

"We've circled back so many times I'm fucking dizzy. Can we just make a decision already?"

WHAT HR WANTS YOU TO SAY

"I think we've explored this thoroughly. Perhaps we're ready to move forward with a decision?"

THE CORPORATE DICTIONARY

Circle-back (v.): To avoid making decisions by perpetually revisiting the same topic until everyone gives up.

28. The Slack Status Games

"I see you're 'away' but responding instantly. Just admit you don't want to talk to anyone, coward."

"I notice you might be busy. Feel free to respond when you have a moment!"

Away-status (n.): A digital "Do Not Disturb" sign that everyone ignores anyway.

29. The Lunch Meeting

"Can't I eat my sad desk salad in peace? Why must every moment be 'productive'?"

WHAT HR WANTS YOU TO SAY

"I typically use lunch to recharge. Could we find another time that works for both of us?"

THE CORPORATE DICTIONARY

Lunch-and-learn (n.): A cruel practice where free pizza is exchanged for your soul and lunch break.

30. The Jargon Overload

"Stop trying to 'leverage our core competencies.' Just say what you mean!"

WHAT HR WANTS YOU TO SAY

"Could you help me understand that in more concrete terms? I want to ensure I'm aligned with your vision."

THE CORPORATE DICTIONARY

Leverage (v.): A fancy way of saying "use" that makes you sound like a business robot.

31. The Monday Morning Energy

"Why are you so cheerful? It's Monday. Show some respect for the collective misery."

WHAT HR WANTS YOU TO SAY

"Good morning! You seem energized today. Coffee must be extra strong!"

THE CORPORATE DICTIONARY

Monday-person (n.): An alien life form that derives energy from others' suffering.

32. The Vacation Request

"It's MY vacation time. Why do I need to justify wanting to escape this place?"

WHAT HR WANTS YOU TO SAY

"I'm planning to use some of my accrued time off. I'll ensure all my projects are covered."

THE CORPORATE DICTIONARY

PTO (n.): Paid Time Off that comes with so much guilt you'd rather just keep working.

33. The Reply Time Expectations

"You sent this email 5 minutes ago. Chill the fuck out with the follow-ups!"

WHAT HR WANTS YOU TO SAY

"I see your message and will respond as soon as I've had a chance to give it proper attention."

THE CORPORATE DICTIONARY

ASAP (adv.): A timestamp that means "I should have done this last week but just remembered."

34. The Process Improvement

"The process isn't broken. You're just adding more stupid steps to justify your existence."

WHAT HR WANTS YOU TO SAY

"I appreciate the focus on optimization. How do we measure if these changes improve efficiency?"

THE CORPORATE DICTIONARY

Process-improvement (n.): Making simple tasks complicated so managers have something to manage.

35. The All-Hands Meeting

"Oh great, another meeting where executives talk at us about shit that doesn't affect my daily life."

WHAT HR WANTS YOU TO SAY

"Looking forward to hearing about the company direction and how our team contributes to the bigger picture."

THE CORPORATE DICTIONARY

All-hands (n.): A meeting where all hands are present but no brains are engaged.

36. The Exit Interview

"NOW you want to know what I think? Where was this interest for the past three years?"

WHAT HR WANTS YOU TO SAY

"I appreciate the opportunity to share feedback that might help improve the experience for future employees."

THE CORPORATE DICTIONARY

Exit-interview (n.): A too-late attempt to fix problems for someone else because fixing them for you was too hard.

37. The Budget Constraints

"So we can't afford basic supplies but the CEO got another bonus? Make it make sense!"

WHAT HR WANTS YOU TO SAY

"I understand we're working within constraints. How can we creatively solve this resource challenge?"

THE CORPORATE DICTIONARY

Budget-freeze (n.): When money magically disappears for everything except executive compensation.

38. The "Other Duties as Assigned"

"This wasn't in my job description! When did I become responsible for literally everything?"

WHAT HR WANTS YOU TO SAY

"I'm happy to help! Could we discuss how this fits with my current priorities?"

THE CORPORATE DICTIONARY

Other-duties (n.): A contractual loophole that turns one job into seventeen.

39. The Office Gossip

"I don't care who's dating who or who's getting fired. I just want to do my work and leave!"

WHAT HR WANTS YOU TO SAY

"Thanks for sharing, but I try to stay focused on work-related discussions."

THE CORPORATE DICTIONARY

Water-cooler-talk (n.): Where productivity goes to die and rumors are born.

40. The Recognition Program

"A $5 Starbucks card for saving the company thousands? Wow, don't break the bank!"

WHAT HR WANTS YOU TO SAY

"It's nice to see our contributions recognized. Every gesture of appreciation matters!"

THE CORPORATE DICTIONARY

Employee-appreciation (n.): The art of saying thank you without actually paying you more.

41. The Working From Home Debate

"I was more productive at home and you know it. Stop pretending this is about 'collaboration.'"

WHAT HR WANTS YOU TO SAY

"I've found great success with our hybrid model. Could we explore what arrangement optimizes productivity?"

THE CORPORATE DICTIONARY

Hybrid-work (n.): A compromise where nobody is happy but everyone pretends to be.

42. The Software Update

"Another fucking update that changes everything I knew how to do? I hate technology!"

WHAT HR WANTS YOU TO SAY

"I see we have new features to explore. Will there be training to help us maximize the benefits?"

THE CORPORATE DICTIONARY

Update (n.): A process that fixes things that weren't broken and breaks things that were working.

43. The Parking Situation

"I pay HOW MUCH to park at my own job? This is legalized robbery!"

WHAT HR WANTS YOU TO SAY

"I'm wondering if the company has explored any parking alternatives or subsidies for employees?"

THE CORPORATE DICTIONARY

Parking-pass (n.): A monthly fee for the privilege of coming to a place you don't want to be.

44. The "Quick Sync"

"There's no such thing as a quick sync. This is going to derail my entire morning, isn't it?"

WHAT HR WANTS YOU TO SAY

"I'd be happy to sync up! How much time should I block on my calendar?"

THE CORPORATE DICTIONARY

Sync (v.): To interrupt someone's workflow under the guise of alignment.

45. The Office Renovations

"Great, you painted the walls and bought beanbags. How about fixing the actual problems instead?"

WHAT HR WANTS YOU TO SAY

"The new space looks fresh! I'm curious how these changes will enhance our daily work experience."

THE CORPORATE DICTIONARY

Renovation (n.): Spending money on aesthetics while ignoring fundamental issues like proper ventilation or working printers.

46. The Email Signature Wars

"Your email signature is longer than your actual message. We get it, you have titles!"

"Thank you for the comprehensive contact information. Very helpful!"

Email-signature (n.): A digital monument to one's self-importance, measured in lines of text.

47. The "Let's Take This Offline"

YOUR INNER VOICE

"Oh, so now you realize this meeting is pointless? Thanks for wasting everyone's time first!"

WHAT HR WANTS YOU TO SAY

"That's a great idea. We can handle the details more efficiently in a focused discussion."

THE CORPORATE DICTIONARY

Offline (adv.): Where conversations go when they become too real for a public meeting.

48. The Reply Delay

"It's been two weeks. Did my email fall into a black hole or are you just ignoring me?"

WHAT HR WANTS YOU TO SAY

"Just following up on my previous email. Please let me know if you need any clarification!"

THE CORPORATE DICTIONARY

Follow-up (n.): A polite way of saying "Did you forget how to read?"

49. The Open Door Policy

"Your door is open but your mind is closed. This 'policy' is bullshit."

"I appreciate your open door policy. When would be a good time to discuss something?"

Open-door (adj.): A policy where the door is open but the consequences for using it are severe.

50. The Diversity Training

"Maybe if you hired diversely in the first place, we wouldn't need this checkbox exercise."

WHAT HR WANTS YOU TO SAY

"It's great to see the company investing in creating an inclusive environment for everyone."

THE CORPORATE DICTIONARY

Mandatory-training (n.): Corporate theater where everyone pretends to learn what they should already know.

51. The Cost-Cutting Measures

"So no more free coffee but the executives still fly first class? Cool priorities."

"I understand we're all making sacrifices. How can we best support the team through these changes?"

Cost-cutting (n.): Removing employee perks while maintaining executive privileges.

52. The Customer Service Voice

"No, the customer is not always right. Sometimes the customer is a fucking idiot."

WHAT HR WANTS YOU TO SAY

"I understand your concerns and I'm here to find the best solution for everyone involved."

THE CORPORATE DICTIONARY

Customer-centric (adj.): Pretending awful people are wonderful because they have money.

53. The Conference Room Booking

"Who the fuck books a conference room for the entire day for a 'maybe' meeting?"

WHAT HR WANTS YOU TO SAY

"I noticed the room is booked all day. Would you mind releasing it if your meeting ends early?"

THE CORPORATE DICTIONARY

Room-hoarding (v.): The practice of claiming territory you don't need, like a corporate conquistador.

54. The "Per My Last Email"

"Can't you read? I literally answered this question in my last email!"

"As mentioned in my previous message, I've attached the relevant information for your reference."

THE CORPORATE DICTIONARY

Per-my-last-email (phrase): Professional speak for "You clearly didn't read what I wrote."

55. The Walking Meeting

"Now I have to exercise AND work? Can't I be out of shape in peace?"

WHAT HR WANTS YOU TO SAY

"I appreciate the creative approach! I find I focus better in a traditional meeting setting."

THE CORPORATE DICTIONARY

Walking-meeting (n.): When your boss discovers fitness and makes it everyone else's problem.

56. The Volunteer Committee

YOUR INNER VOICE

"'Volunteer' implies I have a choice, but this feels pretty fucking mandatory to me."

WHAT HR WANTS YOU TO SAY

"I'm currently at capacity with my workload but will certainly consider future opportunities."

THE CORPORATE DICTIONARY

Voluntold (v.): When you're forcibly volunteered for something you never wanted to do.

57. The Password Requirements

"Now I need a goddamn PhD in cryptography just to log into my email?"

WHAT HR WANTS YOU TO SAY

"I understand security is important. These requirements are certainly comprehensive!"

THE CORPORATE DICTIONARY

Password-policy (n.): Security theater that ensures you'll write your password on a Post-it note.

58. The Networking Event

"I'd rather eat glass than make small talk with strangers while holding a warm beer."

"Thank you for the invitation. Unfortunately, I have a prior engagement that evening."

Networking (v.): Pretending to care about strangers' careers while secretly looking for the exit.

59. The Office Supplies Shortage

"We're a billion-dollar company and I have to bring my own pens?"

WHAT HR WANTS YOU TO SAY

"I've noticed we're running low on basic supplies. Should I submit a purchase request?"

THE CORPORATE DICTIONARY

Supply-cabinet (n.): A mystical portal where office supplies vanish into another dimension.

60. The Collabora-tion Tool Overload

"We have email, Slack, Teams, Zoom, and carrier pigeons. Pick ONE and stick with it!"

WHAT HR WANTS YOU TO SAY

"To ensure clear communication, which platform would you prefer for this type of discussion?"

THE CORPORATE DICTIONARY

Tool-sprawl (n.): When every department picks a different communication platform out of spite.

61. The Desk Drive-By

"Why are you hovering over my desk like a vulture? Email exists for a reason!"

WHAT HR WANTS YOU TO SAY

"Hi! I'm just in the middle of something. Should we schedule time to talk?"

THE CORPORATE DICTIONARY

Drive-by (n.): An ambush disguised as a casual chat that derails your entire afternoon.

62. The Acronym Avalanche

"Stop making up acronyms! Not everything needs to be shortened to confuse people!"

WHAT HR WANTS YOU TO SAY

"Could you help me understand what that acronym stands for? I want to make sure I'm following."

THE CORPORATE DICTIONARY

TLA (n.): Three Letter Acronym – proof that corporate America has too much time on its hands.

63. The Fire Drill

"Great, another drill where we pretend the building is on fire. The real emergency is my workload!"

WHAT HR WANTS YOU TO SAY

"Safety first! These drills are important for everyone's wellbeing."

THE CORPORATE DICTIONARY

Fire-drill (n.): A mandatory break where you contemplate not returning to the building.

64. The "Friendly Reminder"

"There's nothing friendly about this passive-aggressive bullshit reminder."

WHAT HR WANTS YOU TO SAY

"Thank you for the reminder. I have it on my radar and will address it accordingly."

THE CORPORATE DICTIONARY

Friendly-reminder (n.): A hostile notice wrapped in false pleasantries.

65. The Wellness Initiative

"You know what would improve my wellness? A raise and less stress, not a meditation app!"

WHAT HR WANTS YOU TO SAY

"It's wonderful to see the company investing in employee wellness. Every bit helps!"

THE CORPORATE DICTIONARY

Wellness-program (n.): Cheap alternatives to actual healthcare and work-life balance.

66. The Shared Drive Chaos

"This shared drive is where files go to die. It's digital hoarding at its worst!"

"Perhaps we could establish a filing system to help everyone locate documents more efficiently?"

Shared-drive (n.): A digital dumping ground where organization goes to die.

67. The Initiative Fatigue

"Another new initiative? We haven't finished the last twelve! Stop starting and start finishing!"

"How does this new initiative align with our current projects? I want to ensure we're focused."

Initiative (n.): A project that will be abandoned when the next shiny initiative appears.

68. The Feedback Sandwich

"Just tell me what I did wrong! I don't need this compliment-criticism-compliment bullshit!"

WHAT HR WANTS YOU TO SAY

"I appreciate your feedback. Could you elaborate on the areas for improvement?"

THE CORPORATE DICTIONARY

Feedback-sandwich (n.): A way to make criticism more palatable by surrounding it with lies.

69. The Out of Office Reply

"I'm on vacation. That means leave me the fuck alone until I get back!"

WHAT HR WANTS YOU TO SAY

"I'm currently out of office with limited access to email. I'll respond to your message upon my return."

THE CORPORATE DICTIONARY

OOO (abbr.): Out of Office – a message people ignore while expecting immediate responses anyway.

70. The Standing Desk Evangelist

"We get it, you stand. That doesn't make you better than us sitting peasants!"

WHAT HR WANTS YOU TO SAY

"That's great that you've found what works for you! Everyone has different preferences."

THE CORPORATE DICTIONARY

Standing-desk (n.): A productivity tool that doubles as a superiority complex.

71. The Meeting Hijacker

"This has nothing to do with our agenda! Stop hijacking every meeting with your personal issues!"

"That's an interesting point. Perhaps we could discuss it in a separate focused session?"

Agenda-deviation (n.): When someone decides their problems are everyone's problems.

72. The Coffee Machine Politics

"Who finished the coffee and didn't make more? There's a special place in hell for you!"

WHAT HR WANTS YOU TO SAY

"Friendly reminder: If you take the last cup, please start a fresh pot for the next person!"

THE CORPORATE DICTIONARY

Coffee-etiquette (n.): The unwritten rules that separate civilized humans from office barbarians.

73. The Presentation Feedback

"You want me to redo the entire presentation because you don't like the font? Are you serious?"

WHAT HR WANTS YOU TO SAY

"I'm happy to make adjustments. Which specific elements would have the most impact?"

THE CORPORATE DICTIONARY

Revision (n.): Changes made to justify someone's salary and waste everyone's time.

74. The Team Building Exercise

"Trust falls? I don't even trust you with my lunch order, let alone my body weight!"

"I have some physical limitations that might make this activity challenging. Are there alternatives?"

Trust-exercise (n.): Activities that prove you can't trust your coworkers with anything important.

75. The Expense Report Hell

"I need seventeen forms and five approvals for a $20 lunch? This is insane!"

WHAT HR WANTS YOU TO SAY

"I want to ensure I'm following the correct process. Could you clarify the requirements?"

THE CORPORATE DICTIONARY

Expense-process (n.): A system designed to make you give up and pay for everything yourself.

76. The Mandatory Fun Survey

"No, I don't want to rate my happiness on a scale of 1-10. I'm at work, what do you think?"

"I appreciate the opportunity to provide feedback about our workplace culture."

Engagement-survey (n.): A questionnaire where honesty is discouraged and lying is rewarded.

77. The Desk Decorator

"Your desk looks like a fucking shrine. This is an office, not your living room!"

WHAT HR WANTS YOU TO SAY

"You've really personalized your space! It must help you feel comfortable."

THE CORPORATE DICTIONARY

Desk-personalization (n.): The act of marking territory with inspirational quotes and plant corpses.

78. The Office Martyr

"We get it, you stayed late. Want a medal for poor time management?"

WHAT HR WANTS YOU TO SAY

"It's important to maintain work–life balance. Is there anything we can help redistribute?"

THE CORPORATE DICTIONARY

Workaholic-humble-brag (n.): Complaining about overwork while secretly loving the martyrdom.

79. The Tech Stack Nightmare

"We need seventeen different apps to do one simple task? This is technological torture!"

WHAT HR WANTS YOU TO SAY

"I'm curious about streamlining our tech stack. Could we explore integration options?"

THE CORPORATE DICTIONARY

App-explosion (n.): When every problem gets a new software solution instead of actual solutions.

80. The Birthday Collection

"Another $20 for someone I've never spoken to? This is getting expensive!"

WHAT HR WANTS YOU TO SAY

"Thanks for organizing! I'll contribute what I can."

THE CORPORATE DICTIONARY

Office-collection (n.): Mandatory charity for people you barely know.

81. The Leaving Card

"What the fuck do I write? 'Congrats on escaping'? 'Take me with you'?"

"Best wishes on your next adventure! You'll be missed."

Farewell-card (n.): A document where everyone writes the same generic message.

82. The Printer Jam

"Paper jam in tray 2? I'll jam something in tray 2 if this doesn't start working!"

WHAT HR WANTS YOU TO SAY

"The printer seems to be having issues. Has anyone successfully cleared this type of jam?"

THE CORPORATE DICTIONARY

Paper-jam (n.): The printer's way of reminding you who's really in charge.

83. The Speakerphone Offender

"Use headphones! Nobody wants to hear both sides of your boring conversation!"

WHAT HR WANTS YOU TO SAY

"Would you mind taking that off speaker? It's a bit distracting for those nearby."

THE CORPORATE DICTIONARY

Speakerphone-abuse (n.): Audio terrorism committed by the office's most oblivious resident.

84. The Long Email Chain

"This email chain is longer than my thesis. Can someone just make a fucking decision?"

WHAT HR WANTS YOU TO SAY

"Perhaps we could summarize the key points and move toward a resolution?"

THE CORPORATE DICTIONARY

Email-novel (n.): A chain that started with a simple question and became War and Peace.

85. The Surprise Deadline

"Oh, you need this yesterday? Let me fire up my time machine, asshole!"

WHAT HR WANTS YOU TO SAY

"I want to set realistic expectations. Given the timeline, what's the minimum viable deliverable?"

THE CORPORATE DICTIONARY

Yesterday (adv.): When poor planning becomes your emergency.

86. The New Initiative Rollout

"Another transformation? The last five transformations transformed nothing!"

WHAT HR WANTS YOU TO SAY

"I'm interested to see how this new approach builds on our previous learnings."

THE CORPORATE DICTIONARY

Transformation (n.): Rearranging deck chairs on the corporate Titanic.

87. The Status Update Request

"The status is the same as yesterday: still working, still hate it here."

"Progress is on track. I'll flag any issues if they arise."

THE CORPORATE DICTIONARY

Status-update (n.): Proof that your manager has nothing better to do than micromanage.

88. The Clean Desk Policy

"My organized chaos works for me. Stop trying to control how I arrange my shit!"

"I understand the importance of a professional appearance. I'll ensure my area meets standards."

Clean-desk (n.): A policy created by people who don't actually do any work at their desks.

89. The Elevator Small Talk

"Please don't talk to me. We're trapped in a metal box, not at a social mixer!"

"Morning! Busy day ahead?"

Elevator-chat (n.): Forced conversation in an inescapable space, aka workplace torture.

90. The Final Email of the Day

YOUR INNER VOICE

"Stop emailing me at 4:59! I'm mentally already on my couch!"

WHAT HR WANTS YOU TO SAY

"I'll review this first thing tomorrow morning and provide a thorough response."

THE CORPORATE DICTIONARY

EOD (abbr.): End of Day – a flexible concept that somehow always means "right fucking now."

Ready For More Fun?
(Of course you do)

Enjoyed this guide to corporate survival? Your journey to laughing out loud isn't over yet.

Check out these books:

HR Stamped Ways to Tell Coworkers They're Stupid
Your field guide to office species – from the Question Hydra to the Guardian of Tupperware.

And when you need a break from office politics...

150 Puzzles While You Poop
Proven Ways to Unleash Bursts of Genius on Your Throne

<u>More humor books and fun activity books coming soon!</u>
<u>(We know you need them to stay sane)</u>

Find all our books at major online bookstores!

www.ingramcontent.com/pod-product-compliance
Lightning Source LLC
Chambersburg PA
CBHW071213120626
46546CB00006B/2535